# BE THE
# FLOWER

*Life Lessons Taught By Nature*

Find Your Personal
Harmony ---
Regardless +
Be The Flower!
Cherie Kretsch
8/2020

**Be the Flower**
By Cheri Henke Kretsch

Publisher's Cataloging-In-Publication Data
(Prepared by The Donohue Group, Inc.)

Names: Kretsch, Cheri Henke, author.
Title: Be the Flower / Cheri Henke Kretsch.
Description: [Littleton, Colorado] : [Natural Lessons, LLC], [2019] | Series: Life lessons taught by nature ; [book 3]
Identifiers: ISBN 9781732913547 | ISBN 9781732913554 (ebook)
Subjects: LCSH: Flowers--Psychological aspects. | Flowers--Poetry. | Flowers--Pictorial works. | Conduct of life. | Fortitude. | Peace of mind.
Classification: LCC BF353.5.N37 K743 2019 (print) | LCC BF353.5.N37 (ebook) | DDC 155.91--dc23

Library of Congress Control Number: 2019913617

www.natural-lessons.com

# BE THE
# FLOWER

*Life Lessons Taught By Nature*

## CHERI HENKE KRETSCH

## *Dedication*

*e The Flower* is a book about finding peace and harmony in our own lives while encountering difficulties. From those we love the most come our greatest challenges and our greatest joys. As a family, we have shared the most intense tears, from our sadness to our uncontrolled belly laughter. Of course, we prefer the laughter. But the sadness and frustrations have been there, too. It's all part of the puzzle in understanding each other.

I just want to thank you for being my teachers. Teachers come to us in many ways to fulfill different types of growth. I feel so fortunate to have learned so much from my families and Hunts' (my husband) family in sharing this incredible journey of life. I just wanted you all to know that my love is always with you even if we live miles apart, have busy lives, or are just temporarily out of touch. Thank you for helping me to develop my grateful and joyful heart.

# EARTH'S LESSONS

We are all mountains
    strength at its peak
    potential is endless
    challenge we seek.

We are all valleys
    with bruises so deep
    to be at the bottom
    through climbing we weep.

We are all rocks
    secure as a whole
    the pile then crumbles
    new places to go.

We are all grasses
    moving with ease
    a swaying contentment
    it's all such a breeze.

I am with nature
    for as long as I please
    I thank you, Mother Earth,
    for the lessons about me.

# CONTENTS

# LESSONS FROM FLOWERS

What beauty surrounds you
each petal, each leaf
savoring your sweet nectar
little creatures will feed.

Vibrant colors adorn you
stand bright, stand strong
within your group or by yourself
each of you belong.

Share with us your spirit
your place, your earth
each of you so unique
brings wonderment of birth.

Among you I find joyfulness
I'm amazed, I'm free
this joyful peace I feel
this moment just to be.

Thank you for helping me to see.

# BE THE FLOWER

In flowers, I see harmony. I see the balance of color, shape, texture and form. I realize that each of us will see something different as we look at the flowers. For me, looking at a flower bed I see how the flowers are all getting along, enhancing one another, balancing each other—vibrant within different shapes, and tall complimenting short. Flowers stand out—sometimes as a group or as a single flower, but each highlighting its specific location. They all just seem to be *in harmony* with each other. Can you see the congruity, the peaceful accord, the contented flow of life?

The out-of-control flower bed is more about visual disorganization rather than any one flower being the so-called bad one! What may look disorganized may just be a more scattered approach to gardening. The gardener may choose to let a tree or bush go natural or to prune it. Each style has its own beauty. Humans make it more difficult because we all see things differently. We all have different expectations. So we judge appearances based on our thoughts of what makes it good or bad, right or wrong. Is my sense of harmony like yours? Maybe some parts are, maybe some not so much, some we're totally together on, and some we'll totally disagree. Maybe it's how we see through the eyes of an extrovert or an introvert. Or maybe it's blending into a group or standing out as the 'colorful individual!' Maybe it's staying connected but finding one's own way. No matter how we define harmony, it is unique, pleasing, and it feels good. One thing I know for sure is that we'd all like more of it.

Nowadays, it seems like we have so many conflicts, stressors, and discord, that the word "harmony" is seldom used. I think it's time to resurrect the word and strive for it. How about if we make it a goal? Maybe then our relationships would feel better, our jobs would be easier, and life would flow more gently.

I hope as you go through these chapters you'll find yourself asking "What would it mean to find greater harmony for myself? How would I create it? How would I share it?" I hope you'll challenge yourself and set new goals toward your personal harmony. Enjoy the journey!

# BEAUTY IS EVERYWHERE

There will never be another place like this
 Its beauty a loving grace,
So gently unfolding memories
Joy, laughter—entwined lace.


There will never be another space like this
 I wouldn't change a thing,
Freedom in my heart and soul
Empowerment—it brings.

# CHAPTER 1

## BEAUTY IS BEING BEAUTIFUL

What makes a flower stand out? Its color? Its shape? Its uniqueness? Beauty truly is in the eye of the beholder. It is something that catches your eye and delights your senses. If you look up a description for beauty, you'll find words like bewitching, captivating, enchanting, magnetic, lovely, stunning, and tantalizing. None of these words say "boring"! Beauty sets a higher standard. For example: "That flower is beautiful," "He grilled a beautiful steak," "She has a beautiful smile." Any of these comments elicits a superior standard. It doesn't matter how we describe "beautiful," it always leaves you wanting more. We love being around things that help us to feel appreciative, curious, and positive. When we say someone is a beautiful person, we consciously are set up to choose either envy/jealousy or appreciation/honoring. That's why it's so easy to go to nature when we need to be cheered up. Nature is not fake; it's not seeking attention, nor manipulating others so that it can elevate its status. It doesn't need to be the best. The flowers in nature simply are what they are. Whether alone or in a group, dormant or blooming, they just do what they do—naturally.

Think of a normal day for yourself . . . in our routines, we, too, just do what we do. But how does our day change when we want to look our best? If we decide to show our beauty—physically, emotionally, or intellectually—we take it up a few notches. True beauty brings out true feelings of goodness. It's about being in the moment. It's about appreciation, gratitude, honor, love, and joy. When one feels beautiful inside, one is feeling the joys of life, the simplicity of the moment, and the sense of positivity it brings. One cannot feel beautiful and go down the self-judgment blackhole of doubt. If we're comparing ourselves to others, expecting ourselves to be the best at everything we do, or living in fear (which stops us from being our true selves), then we have lost the purpose of what it means to be beautiful.

Natural beauty teaches us how to lift our spirits. When we're down, we can always find nature's beauty because she's everywhere. Stay there for a moment. Take in its uniqueness, its color, its simplicity. Stay with its beauty and just see how you feel. If you feel peace, contentment, joy, inspiration, or appreciation, you have found a simple way to lift your spirits. Find pictures that represent beauty to you—have them in your car, your office, your planner, on your iPhone, and just look at them several times a day. See if it changes the moment of feeling stressed, tired, or angry. It's not meant to take away our difficulties; it's meant to give us a moment of peace . . . or to catch our breath.

Nature—her beautiful gift of flowers—has gone through many more hardships than we ever will. Yet she still brings forth the seasons, or a sunrise, or a gentle rain. Nature never gives up, but she changes a lot.

After a difficulty we, too, get to choose how we're going to change. We get to decide whether to pout and feel sorry for ourselves, or to stand up to see what's new and continue our journey. Beauty is a very special gift from nature which reminds us to stay simple, expect the good, and live in the moment. Flowers give us an opportunity to see hope. They are role models for life. In that role-modeling, we can learn to share our beautiful spirits with others, too.

**Be Beautiful**—practice being appreciative, kind, and loving to all those you encounter. Be in the moment without judgment, expectations, or manipulating. How do you want others to see you?

Create your own flower bed of harmony by becoming beautiful. Or was that becoming stunning? Or enchanting? Or magnetic?

*Be the flowers—Be beautiful!*

# INSIGHTS TO PONDER

1. What word would you use to describe your beauty?
   *Simple*

2. What ritual do you do when you want to be your best?
   How often does this ritual work for you? *Being fresh + polished*
   *shower, teeth, hair, body lotion, shaving, and*
   *a spritz of perfume.*

3. What does the criticizing little voice in your head say to
   bring you down? *I look old, I need to quit*
   *smoking to stop/help the wrinkles*

4. What do you do or say to redirect the inner voice? *I start*
   *taking Chantix and supplements*

5. How do you feel when you compare yourself to others?
   If it feels difficult, why? If it feels good, why? Is it about
   a theme, a specific person, or a location? *Difficult when I*
   *see an older woman + she looks better than me.*
   *When traveling alone, I feel confident and powerful.*

6. What is it in nature that helps lift your spirits?
   *The beauty of it all and it's ever changing*
   *landscape.*

7. How would you want others to describe you?
   *Confident, independent, beautiful,*
   *strong*

7

# LOVING ME IN A SCATTERED PLACE

Today I feel here and there
Scattered me everywhere
Need to illuminate what to do
Yet, pieces of me just feel blue
I sit here pondering day and night
Seeing myself taking flight.


Now a light arises from within
It seems a place I've not yet been
It brings me joy and enlightenment, too
A creative adventure once again, I'm new
It's okay to be in this crazy place
When creativeness hijacks this moment, this space.

# CHAPTER 2

## SCATTERED

When flowers scatter up a valley or a mountainside, we are left wondering how they spread like that—they seem to be all over the place. We love to see that occasionally, but too much of it and we find ourselves feeling busy and chaotic. Like the scattered flowers, we human beings can also get scattered. Often, when we think of someone being scattered, we think of it as a problem or a disadvantage. Many artists are viewed as scattered and lacking focus. Yet these scattered artists have a creative intensity and focus which can be maintained for hours and even days. Sometimes they are so focused that they can't do anything else. They even forget to eat. Being scattered creates an interesting dilemma as we sense its negative connotation while living in America. If we lived in other places and observed other cultures, we'd find that there is a positive feeling toward those who "go with the flow," casually darting from one thing to another.

Scattered people are very often our creative people. They get constant information from their five acute senses, all at the same time. Just think—if you were working on a project in your office and someone came in for help, you'd likely respond and help them. Now bring in five different people all needing your attention at once. How do you decide what to do or who is the priority? Kind of tough, huh? That's what a creative person feels—it's all those sensory thoughts and feelings at once. Each sensory input pulls at them equally at the same time.

Creativity is a valuable trait to have. We don't want to lose it or give it up. It just needs a little direction. Being creatively scattered challenges the person to see more, feel more, learn more, and be more. Who wouldn't like that stimulation? Major food for the brain to play with! Not only does it challenge the person, but it encourages out-of-the-box thinking. Creativity is about innovation. It's taking something further than one thought possible. It is one of the highest forms of freedom. Just imagine letting your thoughts go wherever they want to go. Think about whatever comes to mind, change mid-stream to something else, or jump to dreams of future possibilities—"What if?" Being scattered can truly be a beautiful gift. If, however, it becomes stressful then reigning it in is necessary. Being scattered should never come at the cost of one's health or well-being.

The downside of being scattered is that it may stop you from completing or accomplishing tasks or activities. We all need to pat ourselves on the back from time to time—for a job well done! If we're not completing or accomplishing something, then we'll lose the opportunity to feel good about ourselves. When we can't do it for ourselves, we'll turn to others to make us feel better. Now they are in control of your happiness. How does it feel to hear, "If only you'd do this—or that?" To me, it feels like a lose-lose situation. Now we'll feel drained and out of control trying to keep everyone else's desires ahead of our own. This is the time to stop for a moment and take a breath.

What do you need right now? You have this beautiful gift of creativity and it feels chaotic! Only we can give ourselves true kudos. No one else should feel the obligation to build us up. Nor should we feel the burden of doing what others tell us to do. We have this genuine ability to take care of our own praise—so let's use it.

When we get scattered, the first thing we need to do is a physical activity that can be easily accomplished: maybe do the dishes, water the plants, or take Fido for a walk. Congratulate yourself on a job well done through the success of accomplishing it. When having to multi-task, write down a list or description of all the things you need to and want to do. Prioritize the need for completion. If you can do one thing at a time, go for it—though most of us have several things going on at the same time. Write one thing to accomplish under each item you've just listed.

As you accomplish each step under each item—high five yourself or celebrate for thirty seconds. Move on to the next item to accomplish. Scattered isn't just about being disorganized; it's about taking back your power. We all need to feel a sense of control over our lives. Once we're back in control, we can feel the confidence that it required to accomplish each task. We took one simple step at a time which then allowed us to complete that task and celebrate. Writing things down helps us to focus and organize. Research has shown us that most people will accomplish these lists once written. But I think we need to take it a step further and celebrate ourselves each time we check something off. It's not as much about the accomplishment as it is feeling good about ourselves.

*Like the flowers,*
*Love being scattered! Organize if you must—*
*then celebrate yourself.*

# INSIGHTS TO PONDER

1. What makes you feel scattered: work, people, chores?

2. How do you prioritize?

3. How do you make yourself feel good about successes?

4. Have you ever just 'let yourself go'? What do you feel?

5. What do you enjoy about being scattered?

6. Are there people who judge you for being scattered?
   a.   What happens when you don't listen to them?
   b.   What happens if you do listen to them?

7. How do you build yourself up to get through a long or difficult task?

8. Do you know how to celebrate yourself for thirty seconds? Set a timer and see what happens!

9. How do you use your creativity, your innovation?

10. Do you get pleasure in the physical accomplishment, or in the feeling of pride?

# SOCIAL OR NOT?

I want to be out there, I really do
I want to be inside, alone with me, too.


Social and laughing
Alone—no sounds
My energy depletes
My energy abounds.


I'm trying to understand, I really am
I want all the sides of me, to be all that I can.


A mixed bag, for sure, is what I am.

# CHAPTER 3

# BE YOU: INTROVERT, EXTROVERT, OR AMBIVERT

Some flowers are tall, demanding to be seen. Some flowers are short and bashfully show their color. The middle-sized flowers seem to be able to be both—a bold "look at me" type or the bashful type just wanting to do what they do, alone and peaceful. Flowers teach us that there are many personalities. All are necessary to make a full lush flower bed. It is important to know about these three types of personalities so we can better understand how we derive our own personal energy. The extrovert flowers get their energy from the other flowers in the bed. They love to be the center of attention or the life of the party. The introvert flowers get their energy from being internally quiet and alone. The solitary peace fills them up with energy. The ambiverts (yes, there is such a group) are the flowers that get their energy from both enjoying others as an extrovert, but still needing their quiet time as an introvert; their key is balance—not too much of either one.

People are similar. Extroverts get their energy through social interactions, i.e., talking to others and getting their opinions/feedback. You just can't help but notice them. We feel drawn to them. Extroverts, in general, love social interactions and recharge their energetic batteries by being among other people. They'll have many conversations, each one providing a streaming energy flow. The extrovert enjoys change and can be distracted easily with their yearning to start a conversation with a new person. Extroverts don't mind the open spaces at work, and they like to speak up in meetings.

The introverts revive their energy by being alone with self-introspection and deep thoughts. They love the quiet solitude, love to listen, and love to derive their rechargeable energy from their sense of being grounded. Introverts also enjoy one-on-one conversations that are deep and challenging. They love the quiet world of depth, abstract thinking and philosophy. They excel in the quiet solitude of their environment. Introverts, too, will speak up in meetings, but usually after they have been asked for their thoughts or opinions.

The ambiverts are a combination of both an extrovert and an introvert. The ambiverts are the people that can get energy from a party but then yearn to go home to relax in peace and quiet. They can get energy from listening to others' opinions or by just processing their thoughts while alone, through self-questioning. It can be the best of both worlds, though they can't have too much socialness nor too much alone time. They often make great leaders because they are great listeners and yet can turn on the sales pitch when needed. Most people seem to fall in this category.

Remember that everyone falls somewhere between the ranges of the introvert and extrovert. Someone could be extremely introverted, while someone else is mildly extroverted. We need to understand so we don't underestimate or overestimate with expectations to change someone. It is important to value the traits of all three personalities. Just as the flowers find harmony and balance, so do we when we honor whatever a person's traits may be. We learn to respect each person's operating style.

One of the most common things I have seen as a therapist over the years is that the introvert is told that they need to speak up and learn to be more extroverted if they are ever to find true success and happiness. The introvert is made to feel as though they're just not measuring up. If the reverse were true, we'd ask the extrovert to listen more and talk less. It would be equally difficult for each side to accomplish. Even if they practice the opposite trait, their insides will be filled with anxiety for the introvert and frustration for the extrovert.

Society needs all three personality types—the introvert, extrovert, and ambivert to make our communications rich and full. We need the challenges that we bring to each other. There is no need to judge which type is more successful, or the most likely to be content, or to assume that one type is better than the others. Honor each style—lose the judgment that says that you know what's better for them in order to be successful and happy, learn to respect and value what each person brings to the table, and honor each other's unique personalities. Learn from them so we can walk together to build the beautiful garden of harmony.

*Honor different personality types in order to find personal harmony.*

# INSIGHTS TO PONDER

1. Do you know your personality type: Introvert, Extrovert, or Ambivert? If you're not sure, look up some online personality tests. (Remember that you may have conflicting results, but you'll feel one that resonates more.)

2. What do you like/appreciate about your personality type? How does it benefit you? List the ways.

3. Read the description of your opposite type. Do you know someone who is that type?

4. How could understanding people with the opposite personality traits benefit you? List specifically: work, family, friends, events, etc.

5. How can knowledge of someone else's personality type help create harmony in you?

6. Think of a difficult person—are they alike or different from your personality type? List one thing you could do to improve finding personal harmony with this person, without judging or trying to change them.

# TOGETHER WE STAND

The field of flowers

Demanding

Forthright

This group of beauty

Vibrant

Passionate

All manifest together

Fighting

Strong

We are the fields

Consistent

Prevailing

Together in unity

Voices

Exploding

Significant the cause

Energized

Profound

Together as One

Photo Location: Saskatchewan, Canada.

# CHAPTER 4

## GROUP THINK ELICITS CHANGE

It is awe-inspiring to see a vast field covered in the same kind of flower; the color is vibrant and the space is expansive. Overwhelmed by its impact, you can't help but be moved to stop and take a picture of the impressive sight. The picture at the start of this chapter was that moment! I was so inspired with its beauty that I had to stop and capture it. You just want to be a part of it. Just like the flowers, people move us, as well.

We are all familiar with social groups that have gathered to protest, to protect, or even to celebrate specific issues in society today. These are all powerful messages which impact us as bystanders. From the 1960s' sit-ins, to the Vietnam War protests, to people protecting the habitat of the owls or whales, to a movement to better the lives of women (Me Too), to a culture in need of equality and respect (Black Lives Matter), groups have made dramatic changes in our world. We are moved to think about change. Nowadays, social media platforms have taken a huge stance for change. There are multiple ways we can touch millions of people around the world and educate them on important and worthwhile causes. These are informative ways for us to learn about our world and the injustices that need reform. Group think moves us to see our world differently and to help make it better for all people, animals, and subsequently our environment.

Group think is usually defined as well-intentioned individuals making decisions together. In the positive realm, group think is the basis for new fashion styles, musical hits, pet rocks, or purchasing power. Participating in group think is all about expecting change by using many voices that feel the same commitment. Unfortunately, the negative side to group think, which is just as powerful as the positive side, is when we do things as a group that are hurtful to ourselves or others, such as hazing, cyberbullying, cult followings, club initiations or political/social extremists. Anything in extreme is not good within a group setting. One should always keep their judgment and intuition intact, especially if it's emotionally charged. One can be highly influenced to do things they'd never do alone because the group exudes pressure. Walk away from the intensity of that pressure to make your decision. Using group think to the *benefit* of yourself *and* others can be both calming and healing.

When people are expressing the loss of a loved one—the shared grief of tears, hand holding, hugs, laughter—that allows for emotional support through mutual understanding. Group think can create miracles through prayer chains, meditation groups, Reiki or Healing Hands. Group energy is hard to explain except that healing thoughts by the hundreds or thousands attract each other and create actual miracles. Group thoughts create the possibility of a miracle and the intensity of the emotion determines how quickly it can occur. I believe in its power. One doesn't have to know someone to send a healing prayer. When many are involved, energies somehow hook up and create incredible outcomes. We don't have to understand the whys and hows; we just need to believe it can happen. Within the belief, we create the thoughts and emotions which allow the possibility so it can happen. When many people put forth a like message—great things can and will happen. Don't ever underestimate the power of collective "group think" through thought, emotions, or the power of healing. Change can and will happen when many are behind it.

Group think is based on the power of numbers. If you really want something to change—rally or get on Twitter, Snapchat, or Facebook! Get people behind you—have a set purpose and a plan, then take it big. Expect change, even though we seem to have a love/hate relationship with it. We can see that something needs to be different, hopefully better, but we're also afraid to lose our security, our sense of control. I've often heard the age-old saying, "The only thing certain in life is change." This message rings true. Just about the time we're feeling pretty darn good about life—something causes chaos. Something major changes and the quandary begins. For example: "I'd really like to take the promotion I've worked so hard to get, but I have to move to another state. Now what do I do? I want the challenge, but I love where I live."

Change, no matter how small, requires one to be brave. It's about taking risks. Throughout many times in our lives, we have had to give up one thing to get another. I have a saying in my study that goes like this, "Sometimes good things fall apart so that better things can come together." Though we may not understand it at the time, change prepares us for the next phase of our lives. Change requires us to be adventurous, to get us out of our comfort zone, and/or question what we believe. Group think provides that security within the change. It would be easier if, as in the previous example, many of your co-workers and friends were moving to the same state, as well. Then the risk doesn't seem quite so bad. There is a safety factor involved in numbers. We have a much better chance of taking the risk for success when others are involved, too. The loss isn't as bad either. It's easier to lose as a group than as an individual. The individual has no one to blame but himself, but a group can all share in the problem, helping each other through the difficulty.

Don't ever underestimate the power of collective "group think" through thought, emotions, or the power of healing. Changes will happen when many are behind it.

*Choose your groups wisely—then be the change!*

# INSIGHTS TO PONDER

1. Do you remember a time when you were influenced by a group?
   a. List one influenced memory with a positive result.
   b. List one influenced memory with a negative result.

2. What influenced you the most in each memory (from above): an issue, a person, a cause?

3. Looking at social media today, how are you influenced to both the positive and negative?
   a. How do you control the negative influences?
   b. How do you seek out positive influences?
   c. How do you determine credibility of what to believe?

4. "Group Think" is about change. Currently, what benefits have you experienced from this?

5. How would you rate yourself at taking risks: (low 1 – 10 high)
   a. As an individual risk taker:
   b. As a risk taker within a group:

6. If you wanted to do more or feel more empowered within a belief you have, what group would you join?
   a. What benefits would you hope to receive from it?
   b. What consequences could come from it?
   c. Are you willing to take the risk and do it?

7. Using the power of 'collective thoughts,' can you send someone in need of help a positive message of care and concern? Just think about them, see their issue, and see it gone. Then visualize them without the problem. Do it several times a day or just when you think of them. Wish them well, pray for their healing, or meditate for a moment about their goodness without the problem. Often, that's all we can do. We don't get to decide how it's supposed to look or how it's supposed to turn out. But we'll feel better knowing we did something. Try it and see how you feel.

# NO JUDGMENT

Today
    I skipped
    unknowingly as a child
    and felt no
    judging eyes upon me.
Today
    I laughed
    with friends
    over crazy things
    and felt no
    reason for explaining.
Today
    I felt
    comfortable
    with myself
    and freedom
    to send me soaring.
Today
    I'm living
    in sweet content
    and feeling no
    judgement of being.

# CHAPTER 5

## JUDGMENT: WEEDS OR FLOWERS

**W**eed or flower? How do we know? How do we decide? When contemplating these questions two things came up for me. The first one is how judgment is meant to *separate*. Here are some examples: "You're not my friend anymore!" which means that you are excluded from the group, or "That jacket doesn't look good on you!" which means some people wear it well but you're not one of them, or "You didn't know that? I did!" which means you're not my equal, I'm smarter than you. In fact, our honorable judges make the judgment calls that determine right from wrong, and if guilty means you're not doing the right thing, like most people are. Do you see how we separate one another? It's not necessarily bad to do so, but we need to be aware of how or why or what manner we separate some people from others. I believe we make judgments from our personal history, beliefs, accrued knowledge, and our intuition.

The second area of judgment that I think is important to address is that while making decisions we need to learn to trust our intuition. Using our intuition will help us to avoid the scenario of 'a wolf in sheep's clothing,' better known as *deception*. This is about making a judgment call about someone that turns out to be all wrong, and we get manipulated and hurt. I call these manipulators the 'weed-people.' We need to understand who these people are and how they play with our judgment. It's the Prince/Princess Charming that we can't believe wants to be with us; everything is so perfect. Then one day their true controlling personality starts to come through. We're in a fog, confused about why they're unhappy with us and being just plain mean towards us. They can easily convince us that it's all our fault, after all they're the Prince/Princess Charming. Our intuition told us it was too good to be true, but we overrode it and paid the consequences. This second part is about learning who the weed-people are and how to be careful not to believe everything we judge as wonderful and perfect. The more we know about how we make our judgments, the better we can create a great life with minimal disappointments. Truly knowing ourselves allows us to be more open to understanding what we don't know. The better we know ourselves, the better we can help ourselves and others. So let's talk about how we've learned to separate ourselves through our judgmental development.

There are four major things in play when making a judgment call:

1. Our history
2. The beliefs that we live by
3. Accrued knowledge
4. Intuition

Let's briefly look at each of these and how they influence the way we use our judgment.

The first area about making a judgment is in understanding the influence of our history. Our history is about our culture, religion, success and difficulties—just to name a few. It is all the things we've listened to, clung to, refuted, set goals/purposes to, and set our own standard of living to. It is the colored glass we filter our life through and base our future on. We make our judgments based on that history. It tells us to be cautious (because you know what happened in the past), or to be safe, or to bring on the adventure. Our personal filter also reminds us to celebrate because our hearts feel joy. We get so many messages from our experiences, and all go through our own personal filter. These experiences often include sensory input. So it's in what you saw, heard, tasted, smelled, or touched. These experiences are valuable but also often distorted over time as they are embellished, exaggerated, or minimized. We need to have other means in order to make determinations that effect our judgments. No one avenue in making a judgment is accurate enough.

The second area in making a judgment is that of beliefs. A belief is what we think is important, and then later becomes the standard by which we live our lives. We believe them to be true and stand by them. Beliefs are how we choose to live our lives, and the reasons that we'll take a stand for or against a person or situation. They are deep seated and usually have their origins in childhood traditions, habits, and expectations. Quite often we don't remember why we believe something— we just do. These are the thoughts that we challenge (hello, teenagers), to determine if that belief is ours or just accepted from our upbringings. They can hold us back or help push us forward. We cannot be a human being without a personal history with beliefs about that history, about the life we've created thus far. History and beliefs are the very essence of human life. Our goal is not to try and change them but rather to acknowledge and understand them. It is to understand how our history and beliefs influence our thoughts, and therefore, our judgments.

The third area of judgment comes from accrued knowledge which isn't just about the school we attended, but also about our curiosity for learning. Curiosity helps us to try to see the other side or listen to another's opinion. Our knowledge comes from searching for what we don't understand, while still trying to have an open mind. Curiosity and knowledge help us to solidify why we believe what we believe, or what sets us on a new path all together.

I remember once, while attending a Christian college, a student in my biology class stated that we shouldn't have to learn about evolution. His thought was that we shouldn't waste our time learning something we don't believe. Back then, my feisty side came out. I was angry that someone wouldn't want to learn something just because it's not what *he* believed, and said, "If you believe so strongly in creation, then how can evolution do anything but make your conviction stronger, and your argument for it greater?" Sparing you the argument that ensued, the class agreed with me and we studied evolution. It didn't hurt anyone to know the other side. But I would have felt limited had we not pursued it. That day began my quest to learn about as many different points of view, different thoughts, and opposing philosophies as possible.

I have not wavered in that quest. I know how important it is to have all types of knowledge available to all people. The more we dictate what someone can learn or know, the greater the chance of manipulation. Everyone should have the right to learn whatever they wish to learn, without one-sided information. We are being manipulated if we're not allowed to hear all thoughts and theories about our religion (without fear of excommunication), politics (without fear of having a voice), or family values (without fear of estrangement). Fear should not be a player in someone trying to get all the points of view. The more we acquire knowledge, based on many points of view, the better judgments we can make for ourselves. The venue or timeline in which we accrue knowledge can be different from what we might wish, but general information should be available to all of us, regardless of our culture, our religion, etc. We are all held accountable for what we do with our knowledge. The young man in my biology class had every right to stick to his belief. But I also needed to keep myself in check as I went down my chosen path, to not judge others who are on their own different path. Judgments are sticky-wickets, and we often don't know how to make them work to our betterment and the betterment of others. One way we can learn how to avoid the pitfalls of judging others is to understand our own intuition and learn to honor it.

The last area of judgment is in giving credibility to our intuition. Intuition is that gut feeling, a knowingness that we get about whether something is good for us or not good for us. Its purpose is to give us a sensory feeling. Intuition is that quick first feeling we get about something or someone. In America, we value our brains so much that we're taught to minimize or disregard intuition. The people I have met, who believe in their intuition, find that it's the greatest tool they have. They truly can't imagine not having it. It is a tool we all have, yet most of us have been trained to disavow its presence in the name of science. Because we've been taught how important our brains are, we've also been taught how to override our intuitive feelings. I don't know about you, but for me, overcoming my 'brain-is-always-right' coping skill has been one of the hardest things I've ever had to do—and yet it's also the greatest thing I've ever done.

Intuition is subtle, it's quick, and we need to learn to not only pay attention to it, but to trust its course of action. It truly is very difficult to overturn what we've been taught for so long. Yet when we work at using it, and learn to trust it, the results are amazingly accurate. I now kick myself whenever I override that quick warning sign, because I invariably regret it. We wouldn't have to experience so many difficult situations if we'd just listen to our intuition from the get-go. The fact is, if I can't learn to truly trust my gut, which is nothing less than trusting myself—is it any wonder that I'd have a hard time trusting others? If I can't trust my own intuition how can I trust my judgments? So the next time you meet someone new, pay attention to what you sense/physically feel. If you get that quick turning of the stomach moment, be cautious of your involvement with that person. If you get that little flutter— that's a greenlight to see where it could go. Once I learn to trust my own intuition, I will also trust that I can make sound judgments that are best for me, and for my relationships with others.

Remember that judgment is about being aware of yourself, so that you don't separate yourself from others without a sound reason. This doesn't mean we're supposed to be friends with everyone we meet. What it means is for us to know ourselves well enough to create a less judgmental life. We deserve to be happy, and way too often, our own judgments stop that from happening. If we know our selves through our history, our beliefs, our knowledge and our intuition, the weed-people can't cause us harm.

## SO WHO ARE THE WEED-PEOPLE?

The weed-people, by my definition, are those manipulators who have no sense of empathy and cause us great emotional harm. When we lose confidence in our own judgments, these people endear themselves to us. I can't tell you how many clients came into psychotherapy because they believed in someone and were let down or were disillusioned by the façade that the person first portrayed. Heartbroken with feelings of simmering injustice, they just couldn't figure out how to get through this betrayal. We have all been there! We've given our heart, our time, our commitment to someone who turned out to be a wolf in sheep's clothing—deception! So let's compare our garden of beautiful flowers to a plant called bindweed, and you'll see why I call the non-empathetic manipulators the weed-people!

Bindweed comes to mind in this situation! It truly has this beautiful flower that, if you didn't know better, you'd let grow everywhere. The sad reality is, if you don't get it under control—literally get rid of it—it'll choke all the other plants to death. It's a plant that's super hard to control and to eradicate completely.

It's a slow painful death for your other plants when bindweed is in control. See where I'm going with this? Are you in a relationship that is much like the flower's painful extinction? Well, your relationships with weed-people are real, too! They are painful and difficult to eradicate once you let them in. They know that they've got a great gig going for themselves, and like the bindweed, you're at its mercy.

The weed-people are *master* manipulators, and unfortunately, there are a lot of them. Which means that each of us will probably encounter them in one way or another. These people love to be in control. So the weed-people will be at our jobs as a boss or colleague, or on a committee we sit on, or a new friendship we just made, or a new dating relationship. Their true names are Narcissists, Borderline Personality Disorders, Sociopaths, and Psychopaths. While they are considered hard-core people, we also see a lot of manipulating/controlling behavior with the lack of empathy in those that have addictions, as well as those who have been entitled or overly enabled. Not only are they master manipulators, but they also lack the empathy to care about those they've hurt. They can take us to nirvana and then flip on a dime, walking away like we don't even exist. Normal everyday people can't flip like that—it just isn't possible.

Just like in our garden of flowers, there are some weeds that are just annoying but don't hurt the other flowers. Then we have the weeds that slink their way up the stem and entangle themselves around a flower choking it out of existence. The weed-people are the same way. The more masterful they are, the more endearing to our needs they are. We never see what's coming until it's too late, and then we don't know how to get out of it. The more difficult ones to read are on the milder scale. They take over your life quietly and swiftly because they act so normal. They've sucked us in with their words or a demeanor that we need and like. We're amazed at how great they are. How could we be so lucky to have them as our friend or partner? Yup, they've got us before we even knew what happened. Once they have us in their clenches, they start creating little conflicts or showing us their other side. It feels like Jekyll and Hyde. We believe it's our fault (they validate that), as we're just not being kind enough, or grateful enough, or perfect enough. After all, they didn't act like that when we first met—so therefore it must be us.

We have all had these encounters. The beauty is that once we've experienced these types of people, we never want to get burned like that again. Thank heavens for history, beliefs, knowledge, and intuition! Once you've been hurt by a manipulator, you'll see red flags much more quickly and get out of it much sooner. The weed-people vary greatly in their intensity of manipulation or lack of empathy, so we may experience them through different themes in life: a child, an adult, an elderly person, or a male, female, friend, or a colleague. We need to learn to not be hard on ourselves, even if we get stung again and again. Remember these are the masters at manipulation and our golden key is our confidence in making good judgments and believing in our intuitions.

The interesting thing about narcissists, borderlines, psychopaths, and sociopaths is that they don't know what they're doing—it's just their personality. Their goal is to take care of *their needs*, and their needs *only*. If we can help them, we're important, if not, then we're expendable. Pay attention to your gut—don't override it! Become knowledgeable about the weed-people and the ways they suck you in. Get books or get online and find out about their traits. Believe me, you will know when you're involved with one as you'll feel something isn't quite right. And even if you can't figure out what it is exactly, it will leave you wondering what's going on. Through educating ourselves, we'll realize that manipulators are quite predictable, even though it feels quite the opposite. The wiser, more confident individuals who are allowing their judgment to guide them and believe in themselves will not lose their positive energy after encountering the weed-people, because they know that it's not about them. The confident person has learned to neutralize the impact. Often, they look at this as a learned adventure in self-exploration of feelings. Explore and engage, then give yourself permission to walk away—leave that manipulator.

We have learned a lesson about ourselves and a lesson about standing up for our worth and value. Are you over-responsible, over-caretaking, or over-enabling? If so, you may want to look at why. The weed-people know who they can get to take care of their needs. It's important to understand that no one has the right to psychologically invade your sense of goodness and well-being. Chalk it up to experience and don't go back to them. Heads up—many weed-people will come back to you even years later to see if they can still hook you in with their stories and words of how much they've missed you. Listen to your gut—not their manipulative words! Do not meet them even for coffee just to "catch up."

Just like weeds, there are a lot of weed-people out there, and we need to use our best judgment to protect ourselves. There are so many kinds of weeds. There is no way to know them all—but if we listen to our intuition, trust it, and follow it, we'll have a much better chance of making our judgments work for us correctly. Let's make ourselves more knowledge-able to help us minimize the impact of the hurt. If someone is taking away your positive energy—re-evaluate the relation-ship. Take a step back and be brave enough to walk away. The most precious gift we have is our ability to shine through diffi-culty—so shine on!

***Choose the flower over the weed.***

# INSIGHTS TO PONDER

1. How are you using judgment in your life to keep yourself attached to or separated from others? List according to the following:
   a.   Historical experiences, both positive and negative.
   b.   Core beliefs.
   c.   Accrued knowledge.
   d.   Intuition.

2. Using these lists, write one specific memory, good or bad for each item on your list.

3. Using these memories, list how they have influenced how you see others. Describe how this has increased your fears or your confidence.

4. Looking at these memories, write how they have influenced your judgment and expectations toward others.

5. If you could go back and change some of the judgmental negative memories, what would you do differently?

6. List your "weed-people," the manipulators in your life.

7. What have you learned about you because of how they treat or treated you?

8. What are some of the red flags that you've learned to keep yourself protected?

9. How have you stood up for yourself around the manipulators?
   a. How did you feel before and after that relationship?
   b. Was it hard to stand up to them?
   c. List several ideas that you have about handling the weed-people in your life.
   d. Choose one manipulator in your life and write down one thing to try.

10. Can you:
   a. Unite instead of separate by judgment?
   b. Be brave enough to take a stand for your own value and worth without judging yourself or others?
   c. Make a motto that you can live by stating your new openness and commitment. Example: "It's their journey, not mine." Or "They are who they are, and I don't have to be a part of them."

# A WISH FOR ME

To hear music
>   but sing my own songs

To see color
>   but sense black and white

To be a part of something
>   yet apart from it

To see and hear alike
>   yet different

To be a part of others
>   yet distinctly me

To feel as only I can feel

To sing as only I can sing

To be what only I can be

To myself—Not others

Yes, these are the things
>   I wish for me

# CHAPTER 6

# WE ARE BOTH THE SUN AND THE SHADE

All plants need some amount of sun. Usually, we think of the sun as directly or indirectly affecting our flowers. Too much sun and the flowers will die, too little sun and the flowers will die. Planting our flowers so they receive the right amount of sunlight is very important—it's about survival.

Our personalities are very much the same. The sun represents the need to socialize with others. The shade represents the need to be alone. Too much socializing or too much isolation creates problems for us. The idea is to find a balance that honors the shade and the sunshine in the amount necessary for our personalities to thrive.

If flowers get too much sun they wither and die. In a sense, the same thing happens to us. If we have too much socialization, we lose sight of ourselves, our needs, our own desires. Becoming too overly involved in socializing will limit who we're with or what we're doing. When we give too much time to organizations, clubs, or social groups we start to lose our personal identities. We establish everything we do or say by what the group needs or wants. Our environment, rather than ourselves, is in control of who we are. That's not all bad, but we need to keep it in a healthy balance. Say, for example, I'm a part of a whale-watching group whose sole purpose is to protect the whales, and that becomes my life. My focus becomes very narrow and structured, catering to the needs of the whole group. We won't be encouraged to grow outside of our box because it detracts from the group's mission or cause. While the group cause is beneficial, it is also limiting. We can quickly lose perspective of ourselves.

The other extreme, isolation, isn't helpful either. Placing too much focus on oneself is limiting, self-absorbed, and entitled. We start to lose empathy for others in the world. We lose meaningful relationships. We start to live in a dream world in which all our needs are met, instead of being in the real world. Very few, people can handle either extreme. Think of the hermit living off the land, rarely seeing people, but who is content in his world. Or an actor who can lose their sense of self due to overwhelming admiration. Isolation can then become a place of freedom and comfort. But most of us need a healthy combination of isolation and socializing. In order to have a healthy balance we need to understand how to make healthy decisions by determining who is in control.

The most important thing about looking at who is in control is to know who or what is controlling our sense of confidence. Does our outside world determine our lives or does our internal world determine what we do? Are we going to have anxiety about wearing the right clothes, or do we wear the clothes that makes us happy? Do we join a club because we want acceptance, or does the social participation come from something we believe in? Ideally, we need to make decisions from what is called our internal locus of control. A psychological concept, the locus of control is what determines how strongly we believe that we have control over a situation or experience that affects our lives. That confidence will impact our decisions on our health, our livelihood, our future, and our relationships.

These decisions should be made by you, not by outside factors. I often think of those college-bound teenagers who had to choose between their parents' wishes, for their college experience, and their own wishes. Most often they chose their parents' wishes. So who is really in control? The assumption is that the teenager wasn't yet strong enough to make their decisions themselves. They wouldn't be responsible or mature enough to reap the benefits or handle the consequences. Other outside factors also could have been much more important (perhaps rightly so)—money, fear of hurting parents' feelings, or the fear of failure in a major they chose.

Our internal locus of control is the confidence we feel when we're listening to our heart and mind. We make informed decisions based on what's best for ourselves, while still listening to others. Often that means that we'll upset people who think they know more than us or what's better for us. Maybe they do, maybe they don't—but ultimately, self-esteem is about taking control of ourselves and resolving our own concerns around any decision. Let's say we made a regrettable decision, and it goes awry—we fix it. If we let others make the decision and it goes awry, we tend to resent it. We give up our opportunity to develop our confidence when we blame others, expecting them to fix it. So instead, try to weigh things out, or research it. We learn to check in with our heart, our intuition, and our thoughts. We then make our best decision based on the information currently available. If new information comes to light, we always have the right to change our minds, and rethink our decisions.

At least if it's our decision, we can handle it anyway we want. If we give others the power to decide for us, then we can't be resentful or angry for the decisions they make. Decision making isn't a burden—it's a gift. When we learn to honor our sense of self-responsibility, there is no longer a place to be angry at others. If we use our ability to enhance our sense of confidence and control—then we'll find our balance between our sun and our shade. In doing so, we develop the self-esteem and knowledge that we can handle whatever life throws at us.

Be the master of your garden—choose how much sun or shade you need to thrive.

*Be the flower of sun and shade—*
*Find your own internal control.*

# INSIGHTS TO PONDER

1. Looking at your confidence level in making decisions for yourself:
   a. Rate from 1 (low) to 10 (high) as to how much control you believe you have over your decisions? (Self vs. Others).
   b. List the reasons why you chose that number.
   c. Who or what has more say over your life than you do?

2. List any social clubs, activities, etc., that consumes *too much* of your time.

3. Looking at that list, how much control do you believe you have over the time and energy you expend?
   a. Who or what has more control than you do?
   b. If you were more in control, what would the consequences be to you? To them?
   c. What would the benefits be to you? To them?

4. What do believe is your ratio of social time commitments to individual time? (example 60/40 or 80/20 or 30/70)
   a. How do you feel about this ratio?
   b. Would you want to change anything?

5. If something needs to be changed, what would be your first step?

6. Look at a recent significant decision you made—who or what was (really) in control? How did that feel?

7. What is the best decision you ever made and how did that feel?

8. How much sun versus shade do you *need* to feel healthy? How do you make it happen?

# A DARKENED SPACE

There seems to be a darkened space
    hidden deep within my heart
In wondering how to set it free
    I know not where to start.


What was it, in the beginning
    that captured it so fine
Why is it I can't set it free
    I'll scream—"This heart is mine."


The weight all seems so deep and set
    at times I'd like to cry
Dear heart, break loose these bonds I feel
    and welcome freedom's highs.

# CHAPTER 7

## LOSS OF SELF

Look at the photograph at the beginning of this chapter. What do you notice about it? I notice the wall of rock and the beautiful flower desperately trying to hang on. Maybe it's physically hanging on. Maybe it's emotionally struggling, just hanging on by a thread. Or maybe it's lost its identity—feeling lost and alone. No matter how you see it, this picture is a beautiful flower against a stone wall. Have you ever hit the wall feeling like you've lost your path, you just can't find yourself? Who hasn't, right? I find it odd that we don't hear or read much about it, maybe because it's so common. Yet, when we're in it, it can be overpowering. Day after day goes by and we feel like there are no answers, nowhere to turn—just that lost feeling. While there are many ways that we lose our sense of self, I find the most common ways are due to life transitions, loss of purpose, and the loss of feeling unique. So let's explore—"loss of self."

Let's start with understanding how life transitions can become difficult and hard to get through. These transitions would be things like graduating from school, starting your career, getting married, having children, and losing loved ones. It also includes emotional times like accomplishing (or not) life goals, becoming (or not) what you expected from yourself, or the belief that you're less than average in a world of stellar individuals. While these types of transitions can be difficult, we can be just as lost after accomplishments as we can after failures. One client shared with me how she had worked so hard and then received one of the highest awards at her company. She felt so lost as to what to strive for next because she had just received the highest award she could get at that company. Her fears stemmed from accomplishing everything she'd been striving for. Her question was, "What do I do now—how do I live up to the company's expectations of me?" For the most part, we continue to struggle through the transitions day by day. Then one day we realize that we're lost. We just can't find rhyme nor reason. We're not depressed; just immobilized. This paralysis can go on for weeks, months, or years. Eventually, we finally get to that point where we believe in the goodness of ourselves, and of life again. Maybe through spiritual development we find out that we're here for some reason—so we might as well make it better. Or, perhaps, we find someone or some cause to be part of that we start back on the path with direction again. Life's difficult transitions are about seeing a future—a different future.

Along with life transitions, another way we get stopped in our tracks is by losing our true sense of purpose. We just can't find a direction to go. We see this a lot after a loss through death, divorce, or retirement. All our lives we've had a purpose, whether through our own means or someone telling us what to be or do. Then suddenly it's all gone. If we can't find a purpose, we fall into a very mundane abyss of doing what others want us to do or what we think they want us to do. This is a time when we know we should put forth some effort into getting out of our hole, but typically we're too tired, too beat up or too apathetic to do so. Losing our sense of purpose is all about finding self-worth again.

Yet another form of losing our self is through the loss of being unique. This feeling happens throughout our lives—from the time we were born, through our school years, our first job, relocating or retiring. This loss can be recognized by the normalizing and minimizing of our talents, skills, and abilities. We compare ourselves to others who are better than we are. This feeling, this lack of bringing something worthwhile to the table, is the one that most often takes us into depression or hopelessness. If I have no sense of importance, then what's the point? Feeling that it doesn't matter if we're here or not slowly takes us down the rabbit hole of non-existence. This feeling of loss requires us to find our self-confidence once again.

You can see how these transitions, loss of purpose, or loss of feeling unique, can happen to us at any time. Getting stuck in any of these situations for a short period of time will result in making a negative emotion a habit. The longer we let ourselves stay bummed out, the more the brain accepts that the lowered feelings are normal. If we lower our feel-good barometer to a new low and that becomes the new normal, then our brain won't send those feel-good chemicals to bring us up to our *true* normal. Now, with the new low normal, it's even more difficult to break the habit of feeling bummed out. Have you ever tried to problem solve when you're down? It's almost impossible. Then, on top of that, we additionally beat ourselves up for not finding a solution to our situation.

During any of these transitions, the loss of self is really our self-esteem in sadness. We wouldn't go and tell someone at a funeral to get over it and move on—so why would we beat ourselves up when we're lost and internally sad? How do we move on and start feeling better? Here are some ideas to try.

Being emotionally lost gives us the opportunity to learn to take care of ourselves. Want to take a nap—take a nap. Want to get out of the house—go! Feel like running away? DON'T! This is temporary! The first and best thing we can do right then and there is to listen to our own bodies—our own intuition. It really might be drained—it needs a nap, or a good meal, or a walk in the sunshine. If we listen to our bodies and stop comparing ourselves to how well others are doing, we'll find a place of contentment. If our bodies are physically content, we can move on to our thoughts and feelings.

Our mind is a different bird altogether. The first thing we'll want to do is to start stimulating our brains. A lot of what takes people down is melancholy. Melancholy is a prolonged sadness that leads to boredom of thoughts, feelings, and actions. The antidote to melancholy is stimulation. So stimulate your brain. Take a different route to work, find a new grocery store and buy something you've never tried before, take a walk around a park that you've not been to before, try a different coffee shop, go to an art store and buy a pen of a color you've never seen before. If we don't stimulate our brain it won't create new ideas for us to try. We need creativity to get out of our funk. Start simple—show your brain something, anything new and different.

The next thing we want to try is to watch our words and how we choose to describe ourselves. Remember, the words we choose tell our brain what it needs to do, or how to perceive situations. If I say, "I'm too tired," then our brain must create tired. "I just can't think straight," creates a brain that needs to shut down memory and creativity. Instead, say things like, "I can do (this) today." Or "wearing my favorite shirt today will make me feel better." Another easy way to use words to stimulate our brains is to choose one word like energized, content, peaceful, appreciative, grateful, etc. Use that word to describe you and see how many ways you can use it throughout the day.

In summary, the whole point to loss within ourselves is that no matter what the wall is, we've been given the opportunity to start working our way back to feeling a stronger sense of purpose and value. If it's a *life transition*, then we know it's temporary. We need to start telling ourselves that, and then begin letting ourselves heal from any emotional or physical changes. The *loss of purpose* encourages one to look at new things to try. Doing the old things of the past seldom works because the brain is just plain bored; it needs stimulation. If we *lose our sense of uniqueness*, we need to see our abilities and talents as a gift instead of a burden so that our brains can recalibrate to accept this new way of seeing ourselves. We need to be mindful that the longer we stay down, the easier it'll be to develop into a negative habit. Our brains can form a habit quickly, allowing us to accept that *lowered* new normal. So let's be careful in how long we allow ourselves to be lost.

My mother used to tell me that on my darkest days I should wear my favorite clothes, fix my hair, put on my make-up, and look my best. She wasn't dismissing my difficulty but rather helping me to redirect myself. What happened? People would notice and compliment me. I call it, "Fake it 'til you make it." By doing this simple thing we can start the process of feeling better. We need to remember that life is not all bad, nor all good; it is always a combination of both, each going on at the same time. We need to purposefully seek out the good to find it. Most of all, it's important to smile, laugh, and find joy through the experience, no matter how difficult it may be. Find something to smile about and see how different you feel. Give yourself permission to seek new ways to see your abilities—live in *your* world. When you seek new things to see or do, you can't help but feel better. See yourself as a capable, creative human being, worthy of joy through your uniqueness. Remember the flower that has been decimated by hail, and yet, it will still send up new shoots.

*Be the flower that grows positively, no matter the experience.*

# INSIGHTS TO PONDER

1. Remember a time when you felt all alone, nothing around you but a stone wall:
   a. Was the wall derived from a *life transition,* based on emotional, psychological, or physical barriers?
   b. What emotions or feeling words describe that experience?
   c. Looking back, what was your stone wall? Was it you stopping yourself, or other people, or an event?
   d. What did you do to get yourself through it? Would you do anything differently now?

2. Have you ever lost your *sense of purpose?*
   a. Looking back now, what caused it?
   b. How long did you stay in it?
   c. What did you do to get yourself out of it?

3. Do you often minimize your talents, skills, abilities or *uniqueness?*
   a. Has that helped you or hurt you?
   b. What have you done to start changing things for the better?

4. Staying in a negative emotion for too long develops into a habit. It's telling your brain to continue in that habit. Every day it validates your new low normal.
   a. What negative emotions are you stuck in?
   b. How long have you been in it?
   c. How much longer in the future will you remain being stuck?
   d. What are you doing to break this habit? Be specific.
   e. Are you willing to change that habit and try something new today? Write down what you're going to do to stimulate your awesome brain.

5. Make a list of simple positive things you can do so when the going gets tough you have some ideas to choose from.

6. Choose ten words to describe yourself. How many are negative, positive, or neutral?
   a. Say each word and pay attention to how it makes you feel.
   b. What words feel energizing and which ones take you down?
   c. What's the fuel behind a negative word?
   d. How can you neutralize it with a word that doesn't carry so much negative weight?

# NOTES

# BOUNDARIES

The boundaries are telling
When to go or when to stop
They need to be in place
So my mind can stay on top


So when it comes to push and shove
My boundaries are real
They keep me safe, secure, content
Letting you know how I feel


I stand by the rules of myself
Hoping you'll respect them
So let's just say our happiness
Is based on how we blend them

# CHAPTER 8

## PERSONAL BOUNDARIES

When we look at a manicured flower garden, we see that the flowers have been placed to highlight each one's individual beauty. We don't see one flower overriding or smothering another group of flowers. If we see one flower overtaking another, we cut it back, place it somewhere else within the bed, or we totally move its location out of this flower bed. In a well-manicured bed, each flower can shine brightly, showing off its unique beauty. Much like the flower bed, we can learn to manicure our lives as well. We call this manicuring of our lives "boundaries."

Boundaries are our basic guidelines as to how we want to be treated by others. Sarah Doyle, on an episode of "The Better Life Project," said it perfectly: "Personal boundaries are the physical, emotional, and mental limits we establish to protect ourselves from being manipulated, used, made fun of, taken advantage of, or sapped of our own good nature and drained of our positivity, wisdom and support." Nobody wants to feel the effects of having poor boundaries. We feel walked all over, resentful, and frustrated. We are bound to what others want from us, and left feeling like no one hears us. That feels awful in my book!

While we know how awful it can feel having poor boundaries, it also feels good when our boundaries are respected. We also know how very difficult it is to set them and even harder to maintain them. Just like in a garden, boundaries are clearly defined, but they take a lot of work. Human nature is about taking care of ourselves first. The difficulty comes when we have conflicting boundaries with others. Who wins when a conflict occurs? Let's say one spouse wants to be together all the time and believes that that's what marriage is all about. The other spouse believes that some alone time is necessary and required to have a healthy marriage. This is when we need to understand the different types of boundaries.

Different types of boundaries give us flexibility based on each type's priority or importance to us. There are the *deal breakers* which means "Don't cross the line in the sand." These are hard-core boundaries that are fixed and have no flexibility to them. Another type of boundary is that of *preference,* which means, "I'd prefer you not mess with my boundary." The deal breaker states that it is cut and dry—no flexibility! The preference states, on occasion, if necessary, I'll bend at my discretion.

The deal breaker boundaries are the reason people divorce, leave friendships, or shy away from social encounters. I remember a client of mine telling me about her deal breaker boundaries just before she got married. She and her fiancé both had agreed to the boundaries previously, then reiterated them the day before they got married: 1) No affairs (or she'd never trust him again); 2) No addictions to drugs or alcohol (the dynamics change relationships forever); 3) Never hit one another, ever (she will not be abused). They both had to follow the same rules and if either of them broke one of these boundaries, a divorce was a necessity. I'm not saying that everyone should have these specific boundaries, but it worked for them. They were very clear on what would make their marriage respectful and successful. She had come from a childhood of abuse and elders with problems of alcoholism. The last thing she needed in her life was a trust issue, or to deal with addictions and/or violence. It's not that either of them would ever do that anyway, but when boundaries were spoken out loud they mutually accepted the seriousness and what it meant to them. When they agreed, they could sit back, relax and truly enjoy their marriage. Deal-breaker boundaries need to be stated. They cannot be left to someone else's judgment call. This is about our true sense of personal security. We state these boundaries with conviction and commitment. The deal breaker boundaries are few. So the minor every day, nitpicky stuff doesn't fit into this category. The minor issues fall into the preference category, which is asking for courtesy and respect—but you wouldn't get divorced over it!

The personal preference boundaries are a way of letting people know that something is irritating or upsetting us. It's letting people know, in a kind but assertive way, that we'd prefer they not do or say something. We may disagree or argue over these, but they're not deal breakers—they help us to resolve minor differences that make us uncomfortable within the relationship. We expect to be treated fairly and with kindness. These boundaries are about teaching and respecting each other. Preference boundaries give people a lot more chances to rectify an issue, or it's a guarantee that a disagreement will ensue down the road. People want to be respected, treated fairly, and want to be heard. At some point, the recipient will be held accountable for the lack of action if they choose not to listen.

The most difficult aspect about boundaries is that we need to take an action about what we believe to be best for ourselves. If we state, "This is my boundary," and others are still doing what we don't like time after time, we focus in on it and can't let it go. If we do choose to let it go, then we feel like we've given them permission to not only step over this boundary but our other preferences as well. Everyone's tolerance level is different, but my rule of thumb is three strikes, then I react. Three chances (in a relatively short period of time) is based within the idea of educating the offender. The fourth time is "You're not hearing me, and I will be heard!"

We need to be flexible with many issues that arise in our lives, but personal boundaries are seldom negotiable. Sometimes we slip up and allow a boundary to be overridden, but almost always it comes back to bite us. If there's a slip up, just go back to that person and say something like, "Hey, remember when you did _____? Please don't do it again, you know that makes me feel _____!" It's okay to gently remind someone of your boundary—especially when it's only a slip up. We're smart people, we generally know when someone is trying to manipulate our boundaries. In fact, a common manipulator's method would be to ask us to do something that crosses our boundary—just for them! If we allow them to cross that boundary, then they know they've got us. Once they've asked us to cross that boundary, they'll continue to challenge us on all our boundaries. They may state that, "If you really love me, then you'd let me do what I wanted." It will always be at the cost of ourselves. When we finally tell them to stop, they react and respond, "Well, you've allowed me to do it before and never said no, so what's the difference now?" Now what do we do? They're right, even though we never felt okay about it. Dilemma! We can see the bad position we've now put ourselves into. The solution is to act before the dilemma occurs by clearly stating the boundary. Then act on the hardest part—stick to it!

We also need to remember that a deal breaker boundary to one person may be a preference boundary to another person.

The MeToo movement is one such example. To one person it could be a preference to not be touched, allowing it to be a teachable moment. But to another person who had been sexually assaulted or molested in the past, it becomes a deal breaker boundary. There is no way for someone to know each of our personal boundaries and the history from which they were derived. Boundaries are meant to be discussed with mutual respect. If we know our boundaries and expect others to follow them, then we need to clearly state what they are. If we do not, then we're the ones at fault. We need to state our boundaries before we can hold others accountable for violating them. If we can't speak up, then how can we hold others accountable? This takes courage and strength but will make all our relationships stronger and easier in the long run.

Be the manicured garden. Work at maintaining what is important to you. Take a stand for your own health and beauty. Don't let others trample you down. We need to care about ourselves enough so we can make the commitment to know ourselves better than anyone else. Then stand up for what is in our best interest for our personal security, our happiness, and our respected relationships.

*Like the manicured garden,*
*know your boundaries and stand by them.*

# INSIGHTS TO PONDER

1. Make a list of how you wish to be treated by others. For example: need to be listened to, treated equally, etc.

2. From this list, put them in order of importance to you.

3. From your list, separate your *deal-breaker* boundaries from the *preference* boundaries.

4. Looking at your deal breakers, *who* do you want to be aware of these boundaries? List them.
   a. Have you stated your boundaries clearly to these people? If not, how will you let them know?
   b. How will you approach the subject so that you can be heard?
   c. What will you do if they don't agree or respond?

5. Looking at your personal preference list from above, have any of these boundaries created an uncomfortable situation for you? With whom?
   a. Have you told them to stop and explained that it makes you feel uncomfortable? If you want to explain why, you can, but it's not necessary.
   b. How many chances have you given them to change the way they treat you? What is the rule of thumb, the number in your head that says, enough is enough?
   c. How will you intensify your efforts to have them comply?

6. How do you know that you have healthy boundaries? How are they beneficial to you?

7. How difficult is it for you to take a stand for your boundaries? Rate from 1 (low) to 10 (high). What can you do to raise your number?

8. Before you engage a boundary breaker it often helps to visualize the encounters. It's like practicing. Come up with several ways that you can tell someone what you need. Then visualize every scenario of how they might respond. See yourself successful.

9. Once you've established what your boundaries are, then make a plan, and most importantly—stick to it.

# NOTES

# I'LL BE ON MY WAY

I've wept one too many times
The tears stream down my face.

It's time to set you free
You're no longer a joyful place.

This history doesn't define me
So with sadness—I cannot stay.

I'll keep my happy moments
While searching a new way.

Thank you for all you've given
Oh, the beauty and delight.

I know I must be on my way
Creating a path that feels right.

# CHAPTER 9

## FAMILIES: SAME ROOTS, DIFFERENT BLOSSOMS

**W**hen I was thinking about writing this chapter on family dynamics, I quickly became overwhelmed. Considering there are entire books dedicated just to understanding family dynamics, I decided to narrow my focus here to just a couple of topics that have come up frequently with clients, family, and friends. I'd listened to their stories of victimization, poor nurturing, lack of support, over-controlling and/or abusive people, and more. The stories were heartfelt and had a real impact upon the development of their self-esteem and coping skills. Additionally, problems arose within their inability to initiate, motivate themselves, create meaningful relationships, or give back to others. But their real story was in who *they* decided they were after the disillusionments, disappointments, and hurts. Did they decide to fight for who they were? Or did they determine they were powerless? If they decided they were powerless, or they gave their sense of personal control to someone else, who did they give their power to? Who were they allowing to control their lives?

Looking at the photograph for this chapter—what do you notice? I see the same plant with all the same stems, leaves, and root system, yet the blossoms are different. Like this picture, so, too, are our families. Same parents, same siblings, different people. Really? Seriously—how can that be? How can we begin our lives in the same way, then end up so very different? There are so many variables and answers to that question. Let's explore just a few of these topics a little bit more: family members developing differently, the power of the family unit, and, finally, family estrangement.

Genetically, we were born with a unique personality. It may have been derived from past generations of physical, emotional, or psychological genes. Yes, they now know that emotions are within those genes that can be passed along from generation to generation. That's why you'll see multi-generations that have dealt with anxiety, depression, and anger issues. You'll also see generations with characteristics of cheerfulness, non-aggressive demeanors, calmness, and laid-back personalities. If we look at our families through generations, you'll generally find themes that run through them. Our genetics plays a huge part in our makeup before learned behaviors even start to form.

After genetics, we see family dynamics will influence a person by enhancing traits, both good and bad. This is where we see the black sheep in the family, or the golden child being played out. The family is our first exposure to being rejected or being the favorite, being shamed or empowered, not valued, or being encouraged through love. One of the hardest things to understand within families is that there is no such thing as equality—everyone is different with different needs, talents, and abilities.

A parent may truly feel closer to one child over another, but they will act like the children are equal. In general, we tend to get along better with someone whose personality is opposite of ourselves. We will often see this play out in gender as well.

A father may be a role model for his son but feel emotionally closer to his daughter. This also plays out with siblings. It's truly not meant to hurt anyone—it's just a natural or situational preference. It's the subconscious repelling or attracting. Family members were never meant to be equal. This outlandish expectation has caused more hurt, sadness, and grief than any other disillusion we have. I truly honor all parents trying to keep things equal between their children. But please know it will never really happen because each child will feel slighted in one way or another regardless of the situations or circumstances. Honor that. There is no perfect family!

All families are dysfunctional to some level—in fact, that's what makes great people. Some of the greatest people have come from the worst families. From our rough pasts we learn how to deal with situations, people, and emotions. Once we understand that families weren't supposed to be perfect, we're given the opportunity to learn how to empower ourselves and set our sights toward personal greatness. It doesn't matter whether we've been over-enabled or under-nurtured, everyone in the family will see their life and role differently.

Each of us correctly sees or handles our lives the way we choose, based on our own interpretations derived from genetics and family dynamics. No matter what our parents did or didn't do, we as children will find goodness as well as fault. Each one of us, through our own eyes, learned how to handle life the very best way we could. There should be no judgment toward parents or children, as each was born with their own set of gifts, talents and abilities, as well as a unique personality. Just like the photograph at the beginning of this chapter, we'll each make our own world a different color, even though we seemingly started out the same.

The roots of the plant give it its strength to produce the best flowers and I believe that there are some family characteristics that also help to strengthen each child in order to find their own color. Families can be a gentle net to catch us when we fall, empower us to get back up, and teach us to move forward again. The key word here is empower. Each person has the right to be successful and the right to fail. People who are successful in the long run had to make many tough decisions when they were young. They felt the joys of curiosity, experience, and education. They also felt the hurt that comes with disappointments, poor judgment, and rejection. We have a right to all those feelings, and to learn what to do with them, on our own. Having someone tell us what we should do takes away our ability to learn to trust ourselves. Likewise, we all have the right to fail, figure out a different path, and decide what we've learned from the experience. All of this without someone telling us how to do it better. The greatest thing family members can do is to learn to empower each other. We need to teach each other how to believe in one's ability, to be okay with trial and error, and let each person try again and again until they have found a solution that works for *them*. Stay involved and listen, but don't overreact because the child is hurting. Learn to empathize without jumping in to save them.

As a family member, we need to get comfortable with saying, "So what do you want to do about this," or, "Well, what do you want to try next?" When we step in too soon, we take away the power of the person to struggle/problem solve and come up with their own solutions. We subconsciously give them the message, without saying a word, "You aren't doing it the right way, so I have to step in and do it for you!" One can only imagine, after years of feeling that message, how helpless a person will become. While the child may want you to intervene at the time, in the long run they picked up a destructive subconscious message that says, "I am powerless!" Over time that person needs help making all kinds of decisions. They're now afraid that they can't make a good decision. It's called "learned helplessness."

When a child is in conflict or upset over an issue, let them know that you understand. The *first key* of empowerment is empathizing which looks like this—"Oh, so sorry to hear that, it must feel pretty crummy." The *second key* of empowerment is to encourage them to solve their own problem. We can say something like, "What would you like to do about it?" Let *them* come up with different options, even the absurd ones that you know won't work. Then going through each option mentioned ask, "What do you think will happen if you do _____?" The *third key* of empowerment is to show support by encouraging them to use the option that they decided would work best. You might want to say, "Let me know what happens." Then make a point to remember to ask them what happened. Allow for the freedom for them to do it their own way, without an influencing opinion or directive. True self esteem develops when they find their *own* success. This is the self-esteem that no one can take away. It is the building block toward independence and self-reliance.

So many family members today step in too soon to help their loved one. Everything is directed. Children are told how they should be, what they should believe, and whom they should become. Seldom have I heard that a child was part of a problem-solving equation. They have learned that they have no voice. Later on in life, these grown children can't initiate or attempt anything for fear of doing it wrong. They'll stop trying after one attempt because they can't live with themselves for not being perfect.

I know this isn't new information, but I hope we'll look to the flower blossoms and see the beauty in becoming a different color. There is a reason we are unique individuals. Families can enhance creativity, individualism, positive problem-solving and decision making, self-respect, self-motivation, and self-confidence. Families can also be the greatest influence in creating the exact opposite. Each member needs to learn how to be more tolerant of differences and develop the patience it requires. Allow each personality to bloom to its own unique beauty, feeling strong and capable.

So how do we help each other to bloom and develop within our own time frame? We need to honor, respect, and have patience in accepting that each person is here on their own journey to become the best human being they can become. It's not up to us to determine and judge their behavior and raise the bar to satisfy our own needs or desires. In fact, if we get angry or frustrated when they don't do what we want them to do, it's about us not them. Today we hear a lot about co-dependency and enmeshment. There are volumes of books written on these two subjects so I'll define them in a short easy way, as best I can.

The best way for me to help us understand *co-dependency* is to show it through an example. A mother needs her son to need her, to make her feel worthwhile and important. The son needs his mother for continued advice, financial support, etc. So he needs his mom and his mom needs him. This in and of itself doesn't seem harmful and yet, the goal of parenting is to help nurture and guide a child towards self-reliance and independence. How many times have you talked with parents that can't get their thirty-plus-year-old child to leave the nest? This is one way to encourage a child to become an adult while still living with parents! Unfortunately, in this scenario, the mom created the issue by trying to get her needs met as "I'm a great parent, or I need someone to need me, or I need to take care of someone." Sadly, while she believes she's *there* for her child, she's taken away the son's ability to learn how to think and care for himself.

*Enmeshment* is when there are no separate personal boundaries for the two people involved. An example would look like this: A father wants his younger daughter to go on a trip with him. He treats his daughter as his best friend instead of his daughter. He may discuss with her topics that a younger child doesn't need to know or hasn't the capability to understand. Her feelings are derived from his feelings rather than her developing her own emotional identity. He shares information and emotions that should be for another adult, not allowing for her to be a child. She feels the need to take care of his feelings. As she ages, she'll feel responsible for his happiness and sadness. She has been trained to be there for him no matter what. This will be her life-long responsibility until she becomes disillusioned about their relationship and seeks counseling to help her see what's truly going on. Each of us is responsible for our own feelings and our own lives—no one should be groomed to feel as though they are responsible for someone else's happiness. These parenting styles create more issues for our growing children than any other form. Let's learn how to empower our children so that they become strong and independent adults, not just physically, but emotionally as well. This is true for all family members not just parents and children. We perceive empowerment differently with each family member, making each relationship unique.

Look at the bar that you're setting for each family member—I'm willing to bet that each one is different. That's normal because our relationship with each person is unique; it's not about an equal standard. Next time a loved one seeks your help, try to just empower them and not give your thoughts and opinions about what they should do. Just watch what happens. Some will just go and try their own ideas, some will get mad that you're not helping them—maybe even stomp away, and others will act like a victim and become moody because nobody loves them, nobody cares. Just be kind and empowering, and over time you'll see them initiate their own problem-solving and learn to make better choices. What if they don't make better decisions and in fact want nothing to do with you? Then what? Then we get into the power of silence.

Silence is the most powerful controlling tool we have. Understanding silence and becoming comfortable with it is a huge step in understanding others. Most people are uncomfortable with silence, so we'll try to fill the gap and get someone to talk. Here's a simple way to try out the power of silence. Next time you're in a group— don't talk and see how long before the others engage you. We don't like it when someone isn't sharing their thoughts and opinions. We don't know where they stand, what they're thinking or feeling. Are they with us or against us? We see this power play out with pouting children, teenagers who don't want to talk to their parents, and adults who estrange themselves from their families.

One of the hardest situations for people to adjust to is family estrangement. We don't often read about it, but I can't tell you how many times it came up while doing psychotherapy. Family estrangement, whether physical or emotional is very painful. It is that family member who wants nothing to do with one, several, or all family members. It's the stories of brothers not talking to each other for twenty years or a mother and daughter not speaking for years and not remembering why, but still choosing not to change it. The longer the discord goes on with no communication, the more normal the habit of not communicating becomes. This then becomes the new normal, and years can go by without saying a word to each other.

There are many legitimate reasons for people to stop talking to one another. For some it is easier and less complicated than trying to continue a relationship. There may have been abuse, hurt feelings, corrupt actions, and so on. However, family ties run deep as does the responsibility to mend it. In times like these there is an overwhelming sense to do something, anything, to bring the relationship back together. Remember, it takes two people to have a conversation. If one wants it to be repaired and the other doesn't, there is no repair. We can't force someone to speak to us. What can be done for the one who wants to mend the relationship, feels the anguish or responsibility and yet has no control through the silence?

We have very little say or control to fix this. It falls to the person who wants to mend the relationship to repair their own pain, and then let it go as best as possible. The best thing to do is to send kind thoughts and wishes to the person who doesn't want to be a part of our life. Thoughts are more powerful than most people think. So send them thoughts by wishing them well on their journey, whether it's with us or without us in the picture. It is a genuine kindness toward a human being, whether they're our family or not. It keeps our heart open for future communication. It also becomes a habit of feeling kindly, with warm regard, without having to be physically around them. Especially for those who have been abused by a family member, a thought is still doable. It releases our sense of mending "in the name of family," when a physical meeting or the sound of their voice, is not acceptable. The neutral wish is about us learning to move on—it's not about them! It's about finding a place of harmony with something you have no control over and can't change. It's about not allowing someone else's conflict to disrupt your life, your happiness, your harmony.

Families are our greatest gift. We will be challenged to use every form of communication known on this planet to learn how to speak with one another. Families will give you your greatest joys and deepest hurts. They are the practice field in how to get along, respect each other, encourage each other, and empower each other. Families are our greatest teachers in life. It's not about coming from the right family—it's about learning about ourselves from the family we've been given. It's about each of us finding our own way as an individual and at the same time remaining connected.

The most important lesson to take from families is that we are just one piece of a whole. Like the blossoms on the bush, what we do with our own part of the family is the way we will determine our own color and learn to shine. It's about learning how to respect ourselves as unique individuals within the family unit. A bad parent doesn't always make a bad child, nor does a good parent always make a good child. Many times, a bad parent just shows the child what they don't want to be, and they grow up happy and strong without good parenting. Often, in spite of our pain, we become incredible human beings. It's what we take from each other that helps to create the wonderful people that we become.

Look at what you take away from each family member—take the good and learn from the difficult. Decide for yourself, make new decisions about who you believe you are, and create the you that *you* respect and honor. Find your own peace with those family members you have conflicts with. Find harmony in both the good and the difficult. Learn to be your best you by showing other family members that it's okay to be different.

***Let your roots be in love.***
***Then make your blossom uniquely you.***

# INSIGHTS TO PONDER

1. Just for fun, draw a plant with blossoms on it. Take the names of your family members and put them on a blossom. Now color each one.
    a. Why did you choose a certain color for each person? Describe.
    b. How does it feel when you look at your family flower bush?
    c. What do you feel as you look at each one separately?

2. Looking at your generational genetics, can you find themes that go through your families? For example: depression, anxiety, anger, shyness, etc.?
    • How are you different from your family members and how are you alike?

3. How has your family helped to develop your unique personality?
    a. Positively?
    b. Negatively?

4. Do you remember a time when you were struggling, and your parents stepped in too soon? Not soon enough? How did you feel?

5. If you were a parent, how would you or did you encourage your children to become independent and self-reliant?

6. Have you ever had someone, either family or friend, out of the blue, not speak with you?
   a. How did it feel?
   b. How did you handle it?
   c. Would you do something differently today?
   d. What would that be?

7. If you took action in #6, were you glad you handled it in the way you did? What were the benefits of your actions?

8. In what ways do you consider your family as a gift?

9. What are some lessons that family members have taught you whether you liked them or not? What helped you cope?

10. What makes you a great family member?

11. How are you helpful to other family members?

12. How do you stand out from your family as your own blossom?

# FATHER, HOW DO I SAY GOODBYE?

O Father, how do I say goodbye
To a lifestyle so respectful?
Joys and wonderment abounding
    A place held so sacred.

O Father, how do I say goodbye
To all you freely taught me
Unique and inspiring curiosities
    A place held so warmly.

O Father, how do I say goodbye
To the only piece left of you
A cherished gift of loving memories
    A place held so deeply.

O Father, how do I say goodbye
To the place we loved as family
The only place where we were whole
    Oh, How Do I Say Goodbye?

# CHAPTER 10

## CIRCLE OF LIFE: LEARNING ABOUT LOSS

This is a chapter that is difficult for all of us, yet it needs to be written. The psychotherapist in me wants to quickly tell you about the stages of grief, and how to help yourself through such a difficult time. But my intuition says that that's not what anybody needs to hear. We could all go and research the "Stages of Grief." Instead, this needs to be more personal and realistic. So let's do this.

Looking at flowers, we constantly see the circle of life. The bud, the full flower in all its glory, and the dying flower. Constantly changing but always the same cycle. So, too, is our cycle. We're born, we're young adults, adults in our prime, we become elderly, and we die. Let's just say that's the ideal cycle. Yet for many that cycle gets short circuited. It's like the flower's buds were snapped off. We're sad because we won't get to see it in full bloom. Our loss is just as real whether it's a baby, a teenager, young adult, or an adult in their prime. We won't get to see what they could have been, their successes and potential—all gone, all too soon. All passings are difficult, no matter whether it's a physical release from a prolonged illness, a quick accident, or any form of dying. Sadness is just sadness, there is no way to stop it from coming.

When we first find out about a passing or we watch a loved one take their last breath, we often (though not always) go into some form of shock, mild or intense. Shock may last a short time or a long time—often many months. While we're feeling the numbness of shock, we can go about our daily tasks, but we just can't seem to cry or feel the deep sadness that we think we should feel. Our brains were designed to protect us, so it won't let us feel all the impact at once. It has often been said that if we had to feel all that loss at one time, we would have a difficult time surviving. So be kind to yourself and allow the brain to do what it will do. Have faith that it will allow your grief when it feels you're ready to handle it.

We need to remember that each loss will be different in intensity, in emotion, and in the length of grieving time. In grief, *every* feeling is heightened, including sadness, irritability, and frustration, as well as laughter, immense love, and joy. We can feel the injustice and loneliness while functioning in a world that carries on. People still go to work, hug their children with laughter, play a game, and go out to dinner. Our sadness is that we no longer get to do that with our loved one. Everything we knew instantly changed. It takes a while to wrap our heads around this loss, much less our hearts. Our heads will always lead our hearts. We can rationalize our healing much faster than we can feel our way through the loss.

I don't believe that any trauma or loss is ever grieved once and then gone forever. At each new phase in our lives we're given a new opportunity, perhaps in a different way, to grieve it again at a deeper level of understanding. For example, when I got married, I was sad that my dad couldn't walk me down the aisle. The event made me wonder what he would have been like and made me sad that he couldn't be there to share in my joy. Each event gives us the opportunity to feel our love for them at a deeper level. We will always miss them, cherish our memories, and be appreciative that they were a part of our lives, even if we were with them for a short time. When talking about a passing, I have never had anyone ever say to me, "I wish that person had never been in my life." At each deeper level we're given the ability to love and honor them at that same level regardless of any disconnect we may have had with them. Even with people we've disliked, there's a peace about their absence, a thankfulness or relief that they're no longer in our current lives. With time and self-empowerment, an automatic softening toward them occurs, because they no longer have a way to affect us. It doesn't mean we'll like them or what they did or what they stood for, but we can neutralize the anger toward them. We can find our own peace about the fact that it was their journey and their subsequent consequences based on their life decisions. We don't have to remain in that anger—we can choose personal peace. Even the most difficult people teach us about ourselves; they help us clarify who we are, what we stand for, and how we can help others. Often I have heard clients say how they became better people because of their decision *not* to be like the person that caused them harm.

With grieving comes heartfelt physical, emotional and spiritual pain. We don't like the pain, but it seems like a small price to pay in order to have had the time with our loved one. I used to tell my grieving clients that the amount of pain one feels is equal to the amount of love they shared. We wouldn't want to give up that love we felt, even if doing so removed the pain. In being human, we all know that at some point people we love will leave us through death. We don't like to think about it, but we all know it. Knowing that each loss will feel different, we can't even compare one loss to another. We need to allow for healing to come at its own unique pace. The good news is that one day that pain will be filled with gratitude and appreciation of the life and times we've shared with them.

Grief creates its own general symptoms, as well as some symptoms that are very specific to the grieving individual. One general symptom is that we can only hear what we hear, when we're ready to hear it. I remember at my brother's funeral a lovely lady came up to me and said, "It's just not fair when the good die young." I know now that she was saying that it wasn't fair that he died so young, that he was a good person, and the potential of goodness created by him was gone. But, in that moment I almost replied, "I'm still here, so am I not a good person." She would have been embarrassed had I said that to her—thankfully I didn't. We can interpret things differently than how they were meant. At the time, I was angry that my athletic brother, only thirty-four years old, shockingly died from a rattlesnake bite. People didn't know what to say to us—their hearts hurt, too. They just wanted us to know that they cared about us and the one we just lost. In a short time, I understood what she had said and was grateful for her comment. I knew then that her heart was breaking, and she just wanted us to know what a true loss it was.

Often, we're not sure what to say to a grieving person. Many people are afraid to say the wrong thing or worry that they'll say something inappropriate. So they will avoid the grieving person. That truly is the hardest thing for a grieving person to understand—avoidance. Often, that avoidance can lead to isolation; they already feel so all alone. How many times have we heard, "No one calls or comes to see me—it's like I've dropped off the planet." My suggestion at the funeral is to just give them a simple hug or shake your head in disbelief—show your caring through your eyes. You don't have to say anything. If you'd like to say something to grieving family members, just say "I'm so sorry, I thought he/she was an amazing person." If there's time and you're in an appropriate place, share a story to back up why you thought they were amazing. Just a simple gesture of kindness says it all. I like to send flowers or a card during that three month period after a death, just to let them know that I'm still thinking of them. As we gradually process our loss, and become more capable of understanding, moving into a place of gratitude, we will truly be grateful for all that's been shared, and the caring behind it.

As much as we want to rationalize death—it is never explainable, whether young or old. It just hurts, even if you've been preparing for it for a while, perhaps through an illness. I've always found it odd that in America we're given a week off from work, if you're lucky, to grieve a family member. But when we go back, the expectation is that we're like who we were before the death occurred.

Just know that there are some things that may be more difficult for a while. We may have a hard time with memory recall—you know, those things that you know you know but just can't bring them up to your lips. It's our memory retrieval system that gets stuck in the fog. We may also notice that we need to read statements several times to make it stick in our memory. Months down the road, we may start tearing up out of the blue, for seemingly no reason, or become despondent, even when the day was going well. Even to maintain our focus becomes a challenge. Our spirituality may be challenged as we wrestle with our belief of where our loved ones have gone.

All these things are normal though not necessarily comfortable. Emotions are fleeting and more intense—don't make any big decisions while in grief. Remember that everyone handles grief differently. Some need to return to work right away to occupy their thoughts, some can't get out of bed, some go about doing their routines like daily chores to maintain their sense of a normal reality, and others still need quiet time for deep reflection and reviewing of cherished memories. There is not a right or wrong way to grieve. Find what works best for you and just do it, without self-judgment.

In one year, I lost five people. It was just constant grieving. I thought I was handling my grief well; after all I know psychology, right? Yet every day I felt so overwhelmed; the simplest of chores felt like a burden. I decided that my burdened feelings must be from my job. I went to my principal and said that I needed to quit my job—it was just too stressful. Fortunately, I had a great principal who asked me to just put it off for a couple of months as he needed me to complete a task of some sort (I don't remember what it was, just something simple but time-consuming). I really liked this principal and said I'd try. He'd check up on me occasionally, still promising that he'd consider my request to quit once I completed my task. He strung me along for several months. Through his kindness and sincerity, I got to a better place. When we finally sat down to discuss my leaving, I didn't really want to leave. Through my grieving, I was so overwhelmed with normal activities that I didn't realize that I was just hurting. My principal recognized it (I wish more bosses did) and helped buy me time, knowing at some point I'd be strong again.

I've always been that person who covered up my sadness, frustrations, and irritabilities. Not ideal by any means, but I process internally, and time was all I needed. Again, I can't say enough about how each person will get through this process differently. Let's not judge ourselves or others during such a difficult event in our lives. A simple thing to remember is this: grief works its way through us—it's not us working through grief. Our minds will work through it first and then our hearts. We just need to flow, knowing that many strange things might happen, with seemingly no rhyme or reason. Remember that kindness goes a long way toward healing ourselves and others.

One thing I learned while experiencing grief is the need to *do* something. I was only ten years old when my father died.

I really loved my dad and always wanted him to be proud of me. I believed that he could see me from up above and watch over me, so I wanted to be a good person, just like him. It truly became my guiding factor for many years to follow. As the years went by, and many people I loved also passed, I found that taking a positive trait of the person who had passed and using more of that trait in my own life was a living memorial to that person. If I had loved their laughter, I'd find more reasons to laugh. Then I'd look up to the sky and say, "Thanks." I believe I have become a better person because of the people I have known and loved. So this became my way to honor them while helping myself grow as well. It feels like they live on through me. This is just one idea. But if we can do something, anything, we won't feel so helpless through loss.

My personal goal with loss is to honor my relationship with that person, use a positive trait of theirs to become a better person, and then send out a positive ripple effect wherever I go. This isn't Pollyanna thinking—it's a conscious decision to make something good from something difficult. Coming from a life filled with loss, it was important to me to not get stuck and lose my own light. There are many aspects to dying, not just physical death. People are dying every day in a sea of hopelessness and pain, loneliness and hate. We get to make a choice every day to be helpful to ourselves and others. We owe it to ourselves to be vigilant watchdogs over our attitudes, our words, and our actions. If we can lift someone up instead of adding to their pain, it is our responsibility to do so while being gentle and kind.

My hope for you is that one day, when you pass into death, that someone will want to take one of your positive qualities and continue to share your goodness with the world. Find your way through grief. Be kind and gentle to yourself and others through the process. At the end of your process I hope you come full circle and learn to be grateful and appreciative of the one you lost. Fill your heart with love and joy when you think of them instead of sadness, anger, and unfairness. Let's be grateful that they were a special light in our lives.

*Life continues with loss. Understanding yourself and others through grief will give you a sense of gratitude to share with the world.*

# INSIGHTS TO PONDER

1. Have you lost someone in death?
   a. How close do you believe your relationship was? Rate from 1 (not close) to 10 (very close).
   b. If you've had more than one loss, rate them as well.
   c. Now rate each of the ones listed above with the amount of grief you felt after their passing. 1 (low) to 10 (high).
   d. Is there a correlation of how much love you felt with how much grief you felt?

2. Thinking back to your loss of a loved one, what symptoms of grief did you have? If you've had multiple losses look for the themes and differences in how you grieved.

3. At the funeral, what things did you notice about others that were grieving?
   a. Did you notice any behavior that made you uncomfortable or judgmental?
   b. Did you have expectations about how others should act?
   c. What did you notice about your own grieving at the funeral?

4. Looking at yourself while grieving, how were you attentive to your own healing?
   a. Did you give yourself a set time frame as to when you believed you should be done grieving?
   b. What did you do to be kind and forgiving toward yourself?

5. Knowing that coming full circle in grieving takes you into appreciation and gratitude for the person you lost, how have you accomplished this?

6. What have you learned about yourself through the passing of your loved one(s)?

7. What have you done to carry on their memory?

8. What trait or traits would you hope that others would want to carry on from your passing?

# BEACON OF LIGHT

The irises stand in protective glory
Giving strength to all who see
They rise above
Their beauty shining
Showing the flowers how to be.

The flowers look in admiration
Shining brightly for all to follow
They show off
Their colors vibrant
This garden of love, no room for sorrow.

I'd like to think of those I've honored
As beacons that have shown me
Their footsteps
always guiding
Sharing light on how to be.

# CHAPTER 11

## INSPIRATION

The last time you went to a card store, did you notice that flowers often go hand in hand with inspirational messages? Check it out! Flowers seem to stimulate our deeper side. They center us around openness, insight, wisdom, and philosophy. Flowers are about teaching. They open us up to understanding our own beautiful nature. They teach us about our personal mastery, harmony, and love. They are beautiful and vibrant, dancing in the breeze of joyfulness. Flowers remind us to be greater than we've been, deeper in our hearts, and loving to all, in the flowerbox of life. How else could we receive the oohs and ahhs from mankind? Where else can we see such a variety of color, designs, and growth? The iris protects with their leaves like swords, the daisies dance in joy, the daffodils laugh in the sun, and the roses show off their many layers—but don't touch or you'll be surprised. It's magical how we can feel inspired, loving and full of life, just by looking at flowers.

They inspire us. The question is—how do we inspire others? To inspire means that we stand tall, so that others can see our unique gifts and beauty. If others are inspired by us, we will help to educate, motivate, and move them. It means that they look up to and trust the person we are. Sometimes these people are our closest family members and friends, and sometimes they're people we've never met. We can be a force of empowerment without ever knowing the person who has been inspired. They, as well as us, are looking up to someone out of respect and honor. We're captivated by their journey through life.

Both flowers and people encourage us to be stronger, happier, more creative; to be part of something bigger and have faith in oneself. One question we should continuously be asking ourselves is, "How is this to the betterment of myself *and* others?" "If I do this, what am I teaching someone else?" "How am I accountable if they do the same thing, I just did?" We influence people all the time with both our good and our poor role-modeling.

Sure, we can all get away with things that aren't good, but am I willing to think less of myself for influencing another's poor behavior? People are watching and listening, as it is one of the greatest forms of learning. They want to see how others have made it through good times and hard times. A person with integrity will feel let down when they've done something questionable. If you are questioning whether to do it or not, let your heart and intuition be your guide. We are all human and make mistakes, use poor judgment, or become curious with bad results. But like flowers, we can rise to our beauty and turn bad into good.

It's interesting to note that flowers are present at almost all special occasions and events. We use flowers to say "I love you," "I'm sorry," "I'm thinking of you," or "Have a great day." They send messages of love, care and concern with the intent to lift someone's spirit. Remember a child's joy when giving away a dandelion? Remember the biggest smile on their face?

Their joy of a dandelion brought great joy to us. So how do we lift someone's spirit?

How can we inspire someone through our actions? How do we choose to stand out? How do we inspire a child, a person saddened in loss, or those downtrodden with the burdens of life? What gifts do we have, and are willing to share, to inspire someone else to challenge themselves? Knowing that we are self-accountable for the things we say and actions we take, is the starting point to being inspirational. We need to accept that things we do affect others. We have all made it through life thus far—through many difficult relationships, events, and crises. How did we do it? What might other people have noticed about us? Be a role-model, an inspiration! Be an unassuming guiding light. It is the simple acts we do every day, not the large and profound acts, that encourage and stimulate others to grow around us. Our human journeys are filled with people who helped us along the way. Now it's our turn to help others, too. On your daily adventures be a positive role model because you never know who you will excite, encourage or motivate.

*You are an inspiration.*
*Be the beacon so others have a light to follow!*

# INSIGHTS TO PONDER

1. Who has inspired you over the years?
   a. List their names.
   b. Write down how they've inspired you.
   c. What feelings come up for you?

2. Choose a flower and describe the characteristics that you see or feel.
   a. Do those same words describe you?
   b. Find one word that you would like to be more of and use it for a day to enhance your own growth.

3. Have you inspired someone, either intentionally or accidentally?
   a. How do you know?
   b. What did you do or say?
   c. How did it feel to be "inspirational?"

4. Have you ever let someone down who believed in you?
   a. What did you do?
   b. Would you do it again?
   c. What emotions did you feel?

5. Looking at yourself, list ways that you could inspire someone else. Choose one and answer the questions below.
    a. Who would you want to inspire (children, adults, elderly, etc.)?
    b. How would you want to inspire them?
    c. What is the first step you could take to start on that path?
    d. How would you want to feel about this scenario years down the road?
    e. Do you have the courage to do it?

6. Have you ever been inspired or surprised by your own abilities? What abilities or talents amaze you? List them.

# NOTES

# CHOOSING PEACE

The wind
the skies
a new morning high
a day
a time
it seems all mine.


To have
to hold
joyous treasures of gold
to love
to live
more time to give.


A joy
a peace
the harmonious release
my calm
my life
choosing no more strife.

# CHAPTER 12

## PERSONAL HARMONY

Oh my, what a hailstorm can do to a flower bed! Plants stripped of their leaves, stems broken, and the plants pounded into the soil. In the following days, some flowers slowly find their way back to a leafy, healthy plant. Others limp along but are never the same again. Still others aren't strong enough to hold on and they die. Sound familiar? We, too, like the flowers, need to choose how we're going to get through life's difficulties. Hopefully, we'll be like the first group of flowers and find the strength to come back from adversity even better than before.

How does harmony coincide with this hailstorm scenario? The plants didn't stop the hailstorm but they did decide how to handle it after the storm had cleared. To have harmony in one's life is a choice, too. Harmony means a consistent, orderly, or pleasing arrangement of parts. Words used to describe harmony are; balance, compatibility, agreement, fellowship, unity and oneness. Harmony represents a pleasing balance between all the different segments and relationships in our lives. If we are to have harmony in our lives, we need to find a way to work through difficult things that happen to us. We need to find our own harmony within the difficulty.

What I've found over the years is that most people want to live in harmony, both within themselves and with others. Maybe they're good at handling conflict, but that doesn't mean they want to deal with it or even get used to it. When we get hit by something that is hard to deal with, we will automatically defend and protect ourselves. Our brains were made to protect and keep the body and mind safe. This protection puts our brain on high alert. High alert is *not* harmonious. To protect us, our brain goes back into our past to help it decide how to move forward. Unfortunately, it searches to find old messages (in psychology we call them "tapes") that we've been told by others, or ourselves, when we were younger to protect us. Our upbringing helped to reinforce many thoughts that we carry with us throughout our whole lives.

How can we protect ourselves when we have so many childhood tapes in our brain telling us what to do, or not to do? We may not even remember why we think or feel a certain way; it just happens. If we take the old tapes apart and find their source, we often can correct it—just because we have accrued more experiences to select from. If we want to change these old tapes, we'll need to show our brain real experiences that render the message as no longer valid. We can then insert the new thought we have about that experience. For example: If I see a homeless man on the streets my old tape might say, "Be careful, he will hurt you." Having had experiences around the homeless, we've learned that that is rarely the case. So the new thought may be "That's really not true. Remember when you sat and talked to a homeless guy and found out he was just down on his luck? He wished no one harm." The brain now has a new way to perceive homeless people and the old tapes no longer apply.

By the way, it's okay to talk to our own brain—we're not crazy! Our sophisticated brains can rewire when it is validated through a believable experience. You may have to *redirect* it a few times before it becomes automatic—but it will happen.

Finding our harmony within difficulty means that we need to start with ourselves and the way we think about things. Giving our brain a new perspective starts the process towards potential harmony. The gift of finding harmony is about finding personal peace no matter what is thrown at us. It's not about being on a timetable, but it is about moving forward.

Harmony starts with understanding our thoughts as best we can. We personally get to decide whether personal peacefulness works for us or not. If we decide it does, we'll maintain it, making it even better. If, however, we decide that this is not the way we want to go, then keeping the old tapes and replaying them is our only option. Redirecting our thoughts is the key if we want to find true harmony.

Another way to redirect under difficult circumstances can be in *neutralizing* the thoughts. Neutralizing is saying things like, "This, too, shall pass." Or "That's their journey, not mine." A neutral thought helps our minds to know that the difficulty is going to be okay. Then the brain will start problem-solving towards the desired outcome. It's okay to be in the neutral zone or the "proceed with caution zone," as I call it. If we're in a conflict with someone, it's okay to back away, giving it time to see how it could play out. Time is a great healer of events and relationships. Time gives us the space to think about what we really want or need. It allows the space to emotionally heal or to try to better understand the situation. We shouldn't be afraid of backing off and getting clarity. It is a great life-saving tool in the world of conflict resolution.

Finding our personal harmony doesn't mean we live in peace and calm every day. What it means is that we are in a positive position and have created tools for ourselves that are available when we need them. These tools will help get us through a difficult situation much quicker so we can move on to something more pleasant. Redirecting and neutralizing allows us to remove ourselves from the need to be in control of the things we don't get to control. Unfortunately, we have very little control over most of the situations and people in our lives. We only get to control ourselves—and that's a huge job, in and of itself! The sooner we can give up control of others and situations, the faster we'll find our harmony. I can be upset that someone hurt me, or I can feel that it's their issue, not mine. When I put it into my life's story, I get to decide where it fits. If it doesn't fit, it gets discarded and I no longer need to think about it. If it does fit, I get to decide what I want to do with it.

We have the inherent right to be happy. If anyone is trying to take our happiness away, we need to measure the angst vs the joy. If there's little joy, then we need to weed our garden or find new strength befitting of us. No one gets to take away our joy and happiness unless we let them. Only we get to decide what flowers are in our garden of life—which ones make us more vibrant, colorful, inspirational, kind, and empowering. Remember, it's not about creating the perfect situation; it's about knowing how to become peaceful within a situation.

Harmony starts when we decide what gives us personal peace and then acting upon it. We need to decide who or what creates the chaos, who encourages us or puts us down. What are the inner rules for governing ourselves? Who should be in our garden? Who do we believe should leave or stay in our life? Who believes in us and will walk with us through a difficulty? We get to create our garden of harmony! We can have as much chaos or peace as we choose.

When we've created our own peace and harmony, others will be automatically attracted to its calmness. This then gives us the platform to create harmony around ourselves through role-modeling, speaking our truth, empowering others, and complimenting goodness. Only we can create our personal inner harmony—nobody else gets that power. Use it wisely!

### *Be the flower garden of harmony!*

# INSIGHTS TO PONDER

1. How would you define harmony?

2. Have you ever felt harmony?
   a. What did it feel like?
   b. Where were you, who were you with, or what was the event?

3. Looking at the list below, specifically, who stops you from finding your harmony?
   a. Family:
   b. Friends:
   c. Work: (people and scenarios)
   d. Events/Occasions:
   e. Others:

4. Finding harmony within a relationship can be challenging. From the list above, which relationship would you choose to work on?
   a. What makes the relationship challenging?
   b. What would you have to do to find peace within yourself (even if they don't change)?

5. What brings harmony to your life?
   a. How often do you have it? (out of 100 percent)
   b. What needs to change in order to spend more time in harmony?

6. How do you currently project your inner harmony towards others?

7. If you could change a difficulty in your life right now, what would it be?
    a.  How would it feel to be free from worry about that?
    b.  What about it creates your stress?
    c.  If you could imagine it in a manageable form, what would that look like?
    d.  Is it worth it to you to do something about it? If so, what would the next step be?

# A LIFE CREATED

The flowers simply show us
how beautiful life is
it doesn't mean it won't be hard
                    but the strength
                      lies therein.

The prickly pear understands
how the good, yet hard, are present
its spikes of self-protection
                      its lovely flowers
                      of inspiration.

We protect ourselves as need be, too,
what we share or choices we make
it's knowing self and others
                      a satisfaction
                      a life at stake.

Love the beauty of the flowers
love the life that you make
weigh the aspects of happiness and sorrow
                      love the YOU
                      that you create.

# ABOUT THE AUTHOR

Cheri Henke Kretsch grew up as a mountain girl in Colorado. Born as a carefree lover of life, the only world she knew was filled with animals, nature, and a loving family. After experiencing traumatic events in childhood and adolescence, the mountains taught her, once again, to trust and love. Living in nature gave her the strength to go on, the eyes to see healing, and the heart to share. Her love of nature and the metaphors derived from it, developed a life-long gift to help her understand the world she lives in.

Cheri Henke Kretsch is a licensed psychotherapist with twenty-seven years of experience working for large companies, on military bases, and in private practice. In addition, Henke Kretsch has spent over twenty years in teaching psychology; working with special-needs students, as a guidance counselor at the high school level and as an adjunct professor of psychology at the college level.

Henke Kretsch is the recipient of the Outstanding Young Educator Award for Kansas. She was twice awarded Who's Who in Education and was Counselor of the Year for Jefferson County Schools, Colorado. Henke Kretsch has also won both the Golden and Silver Poets Award in Washington, DC.

Cheri Henke Kretsch currently resides in Littleton, Colorado. She can be contacted at cheri@natural-lessons.com or www.natural-lessons.com.

Made in the USA
Monee, IL
22 February 2020

22155613R00079